Can Humans Have SUPERPOWERS?

TO OUR PARENTS:

Avtar & Tej Sivia
Desmond & Patricia White

For raising us to believe that anything is possible

Can humans have superpowers?
That's a question often asked to me.
If they could, would you like
to time travel like Suzy?
Where would you go?

Or how about superstrength
like Steven to throw things
high across the sky....
all the way to the moon!

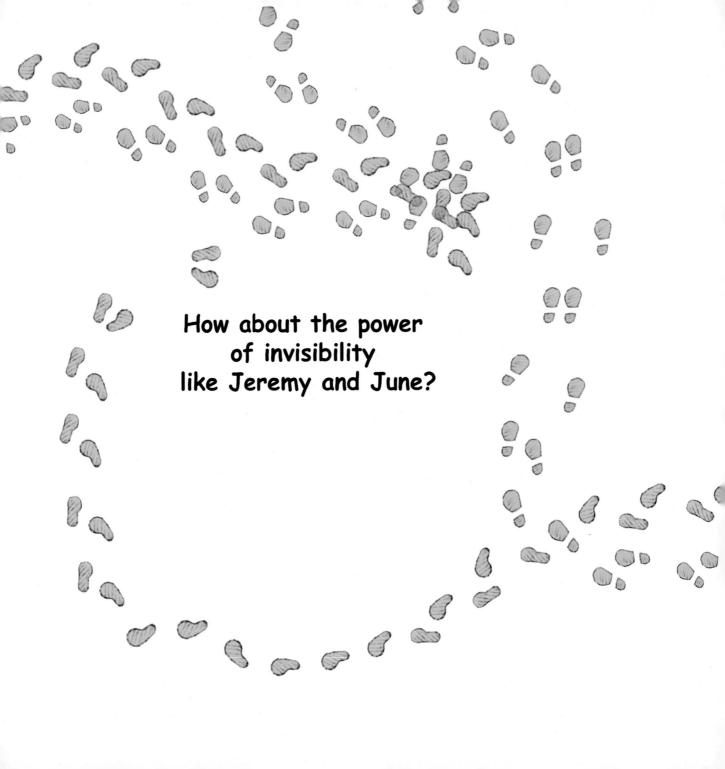

How about the power
of invisibility
like Jeremy and June?

Or maybe you just want to fly
like Fred free as a bird.
Well I got some news for you,
each of us have superpowers within.
Turn to the next page
and I shall begin.

KINDNESS is a superpower,
so lend a hand to your friends like Leo
and help them get back on their feet.

Or maybe pick up litter
on the beach because taking care of
the environment is sweet.

You can even share your supplies
at school like Raul.
KINDNESS is simple and it's free.

Why not join Fazia and
help her plant a tree?

A big and bright smile is KIND
and can make a day.
Now you know that KINDNESS
goes a long way.
Ask yourself one last question.

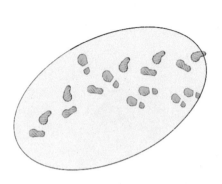

What will be my
superpower today?

Made in the USA
Monee, IL
17 July 2023